Ava Breaks the Rules

Written by Jackie Hull

Made possible By Gem N Me
Penny Publishing Co. 2021
United Black Fund

© All rights reserved. No part of this book may be reproduced in any manner what so ever with out written permission.
Published 2021

Illustrated by:
tullipstudio

Dedication:

This book is dedicated to any and everyone that has ever had a dream. Just like me if you put your mind to it and do your best you can accomplish anything! I want to thank my mommy for believing in me, my DEA for always helping me, my daddy for loving me, and my whole family for supporting me. I want to thank Ms. Penny and GemNMe for taking the time to help us. Love Jackie R. Hull

Introduction

Hi, my name is Jackie, and I am the creator of this book. I'm 7 years old, and just like all kids, I struggle with following the rules. Sometimes it's just too many. Other times it's too hard. Then there are times where I just want to do my own thing.

My mom always tells me these 3 things, 1. Make good choices, 2. I shouldn't put myself in a position where I can be accused of things I didn't do, and 3. I can choose my actions, but I can't choose my consequences. I try my best, but I don't get it right all the time. Is this the same for you? Since you said yes, I think we would be great friends if we hung out in real life but because this is impossible. Can you do me a favor and help my friend Ava stop breaking the rules so much and make better choices?

This book was my idea, but I had help from my mommy. My mom's name is Ebony Jae, and she is a Licensed Independent Social worker. My mom works with all types of people through therapeutic ways of helping them be their best selves. I'll share what I think, and we will help teach you and the grown-ups helping you how to apply Social-Emotional Skills (SEL) to your everyday life. SEL skills are important, so we are better able to handle everyday challenges as kids all the way to adulthood. I'm excited for us to work together to help my friend Ava get back on track.

Teacher: "Ok, class, please take out a pencil and paper; we are going to journal about what we did this past weekend silently."

Ava: Yells, "I didn't do anything, so I'm not writing anything." Ava begins to try to get Layla's attention. "Layla, did you see that one tic toc...?"

Teacher: "Ava, you are not following directions; this is silent journal time. I think you need a time out."

Embarrassed, Ava began to cry loudly and stomp her feet. The teacher tells her to go sit in the "hot seat" away from the other students. "I will be calling your parents," he says.

With a "stank face," Ava folds her arms and walks to the hot seat, murmuring, "I didn't even do anything."

Can you help Ava?

What could Ava have done differently?

What Jackie says:
Ava could have taken a deep breath and walked quietly to the hot seat since she was talking when it wasn't supposed to be talking time.

What Skills Can Ava be taught here?
On your own, journaling is a good way to write out your feelings. In the classroom, journaling helps students build writing skills and communicate ideas. Ava could have used this opportunity to write her feelings.

SEL Skill:
Self-management:
being able to manage emotions and behaviors to achieve the best options. Ava did not use this skill when she did things like stomping and yelling.

"Hey Ava, you want to play tag with us?" Ayden asks. "Sure," Ava says. "Ok, that makes you "it"," Starr yells while running away with the other kids.

Upset because she doesn't want to be "it", she comes up with a plan. "They always make me it, and that's not fair!" As one of her classmates comes down the slide, Ava sticks out her leg.

Armintha trips and falls and scrapes her knee. "Ava, why would you do that? You are so mean; that's why no one likes to play with you", Armintha says in a crying voice.

Teacher: "Recess is over, it's time to line up"

Layla: (Ava continues to run around) "Ava, you better get in line before you get in trouble again."

Teacher: ". 1.2... Ava, you're still not following directions; if I get to 3, you will get your card flipped."

Ava: (Finally stomps to the line with her arms folded, mumbling all the way to class) "This isn't fair; I still want to play."

The teacher sees the little girl crying by the slide, and once she finds out Ava is part of the problem, she decides she has had enough. "Ava, go to Principal Humphrey's office now," she says in an exhausted voice.

Ava goes to meet with Principal Humphrey, where he tells her that he is aware that she has had a hard time today. He lets her know that he will be requesting for her parents to come in for a meeting.

Can you help Ava?

What are somethings you do to let others know you are mad?
What should be Ava's consequences?

What Jackie says:
Sometimes when I get mad, I do things I shouldn't. When this happens, I get my phone taken, or I may get on punishment, and my parents tell me how I let them down because of my actions. I don't like to let people down, and I don't like when people let me down. I don't like to be on punishment, so I try to fix what I did.
*Parents, take time to teach kids that anger is an emotion we all have but that there is a right time and way to show this.

What skill can Ava be taught here?
Having friends is important. We have to make sure we are treating each other right.

SEL Skill:
Relationship Skills = Forming positive relationships, dealing with conflict in the right way. Ava should have let her friends know that she was upset and that they should take turns being "it."

Principal Humphrey: "Thank you for coming in today. Ava is struggling extremely hard. We have tried our best to get her to make changes, but nothing has worked. She even went as far as hurting one of our students on purpose on the playground today. I would like to discuss her working with our Therapist Mrs. Penny.

Mr. Hull: I am not sure about that I don't want my little girl to be labeled.

Principal Humphrey: "I completely understand your concern Mr. Hull, but I assure you that this will help Ava. Sometimes we all need a little help. Therapy will help Ava and the family make the adjustments that may be needed as a whole. How about You can meet with Mrs. Penny first, that way you can discuss your fears with her. I promise You won't regret it. Ava's parents agree to meet with the counselor.
Mrs. Penny explains that with the tools used in therapy, along with the support of the family, school, "Ava will make improvements in no time."

Mrs. Hull expresses, "Nothing seems to be working right now, so, why not give therapy a try?"

While Ava is waiting for her parents to get home from her school, she starts to reflect on her past week. "Everyone thinks I need to be different, so I will show them", Says Ava.

Hopefully then everyone will stop comparing me to my siblings. "Oh Ava, you should braid hair like DeMaria or maybe you'll be a basketball star just like Alex. How about you be helpful like Gabby? You can always be observant like your brother Sta'ce!".

Why can't I just be me? First she looks in her closet and trys on some of her clothes. Naw, I've worn all these clothes before. Next, she decided to go on tic toc to learn some new dance moves. "Oh this is too hard", Ava realizes. I got it, Ava went to the bathroom and found some temporay hair dye and colored her hair blue. "This will for sure, make me a different girl", says Ava.

Ava smiled as she looked in the mirror. "I going to be the coolest kid in second grade with my new blue hair.

"Ava, soon as your dad comes in, we really need to talk to you; please come downstairs immediately," says her mother.

"Ok, here I come," Ava excitedly responds.

When Ava's mom saw her, she was very shocked. "Ava, your hair! You are too young to dye your hair, and blue of all colors?"

"Mom, chill," Ava says.

Ava's mom: "Did you just tell me to chill? You are getting beside yourself, young lady. I can't believe this, none of my other kids…

Ava stopped her mother, and with tears in her eyes, she yells "I am not them! I just want to be me! I hate you, and I hate it here."

Just then, Ava's father walks into the house. "What is going on in here?"

"Ava, we are very disappointed in you. What is going on with you? You are getting in trouble in school, being mean to your friends, and now being rude to your mother.

Wait, when did your hair get blue?" Ava's dad asks.

Ava: "I don't know. I just do things. Everyone is always telling me that I need to change. So I thought changing my hair would make things better."

Changing your hair will not help you follow the rules, Mrs. Hull told her.

Mr. Hull: "Well, maybe you need to sit in your room and figure it out."

Ava: (Laid on her bed and cried herself to sleep) "I don't know why there are so many rules anyway."

Can you help Ava?

Was Ava's response appropriate? Why or why not? If not, how would you have shared your feelings with your parent?
Was Ava's mom overreacting? Is blue hair a bad thing? Should kids be able to express themselves in any way they want?

What Jackie says:
Ava could have said that she wanted to be like herself, and she thinks her blue hair is beautiful.

What Skill Can Ava be taught here?
Kids are adults in the making. It is important for kids to be given a safe space to express themselves, but they must remember to be respectful. Each child should be free to have his/her own unique style. Teaching kids effective communication and being respectful when speaking to others is very important.

SEL Skill:
Self-awareness/Self-concept= being aware of one's thoughts, feelings, and emotions.
*Parents, we are all unique individuals. Please remember it is ok to compromise sometimes. Letting children express themselves in appropriate ways helps develop positive self-esteem.

"Good morning Ava, at school today, you will meet with the school Therapist, Mrs. Penny," Ava's mom explained.

Why do I have to do this when people be messing with me?"

Her mom answered, "Ava, hopefully, she can help with that negative attitude of yours."

Ava's angry response was, "I don't need no dumb therapy. I'm not crazy.

Her dad says, "Therapy is not for crazy people, Ava."

Ava: "Well, why am I going then?"

"Mrs. Penny is going to help us figure out why you are having a hard time with following directions," said her dad.

Ava: "What does she know?'

Her mom answered, "Ava, hopefully, she can help with that negative attitude of yours."

Ava slowly walks into the class. She begins to cry. Her friend Layla comes over to her to comfort her and find out what is going on.

"Hey, bestie, what's wrong." Layla asked.

Ava reluctantly whispers," My parents are making me go meet with the therapist.

" Layla's face lit up, "You get to work with Mrs. Penny?"

"Yes, how do you know her?" Ava asked.

"I work with Mrs. Penny too. I get to tell her about things that are bothering me, and she helps me make good decisions," Layla told her.

Mrs. Penny has a lot of cool stuff in her office, and she is a great listener", explained Layla. "It can be tough sometimes, but you will love it. Everyone likes doing better.

Can you help Ava?
If you saw Ava crying, would you make fun of her? Why or Why not?

What Jackie says:
Laughing and joking with your friend is ok but when it starts to hurt some feelings, that could be called bullying. Bullying is never ok!

What Skill Can Ava be taught here?
Bullying can cause harm to others, and there can be severe consequences.

SEL Skill:
Social awareness = showing understanding and empathy for others. Layla displayed this by seeing what was wrong with her friend and giving positive feedback.

Mrs. Penny: "Hello Ava, it's good to meet you today."

Ava: "I don't want to be here. This is going to be dumb? I don't like it here. Plus, I'm not crazy."

Mrs. Penny: Everyone can benefit from therapy, and that doesn't mean your crazy.

Ava: "So what are we going to do here? My friend Layla said she gets to talk about how people get on her nerves?"

Mrs. Penny laughs, "You will get a chance to tell me about things and people that bother you, and I will help you learn coping skills in order for you to make the right choices. Do you know what coping skills are?

"No, what's that?" Ava asked

Mrs. Penny: "Coping skills are tools and techniques to help you handle difficult things like when you're angry, afraid, unable to get schoolwork done, and taking responsibility when you have made poor choices."

Ava: "Can it help me follow directions better?"

Mrs. Penny: "Absolutely."

Ava: (Running to Mrs. Penny's office) "Mrs. Penny, Mrs. Penny, guess what? I got picked for the most improved student".

Mrs. Penny: "That's great, Ava. Let's go over what you've learned in our session."

Ava: "I've learned that when I mess up, I can do things to fix it. I learned that I could be upset but not be mean to others. My parents really like that I understand that I have to follow the rules or the outcome could be very bad."

Mrs. Penny: "Well, it seems you've learned a lot, Ava. You have worked really hard; how do you feel about this?"

Ava: "I am very happy. Last week I got mad and hit my brother, but I apologized without anyone telling me to because I knew that was wrong, even though he was irritating me. I still get it wrong sometimes, but I keep trying my best, just like my parents and you, Mrs. Penny always tell me."

Can you help Ava?

What do you know about therapy?

What Jackie says:

My mom is a therapist, and she helps her clients and me to be our best selves. She taught me about affirmations. Do you know what affirmations are? It's when you say nice things about yourself like: "I am smart, I'm kind. I am beautiful, and I can do anything I set my mind to".

*Parents, it's ok for your child to see a therapist if they are struggling. That doesn't make you a bad parent or mean your child is crazy!

What Skill Can Ava be taught here?
Making responsible decisions help keep you and others safe.

Responsible Decision Making = Making constructive ethical choices about personal and social behavior.

The End

Made in the USA
Middletown, DE
16 November 2022

14875974R00020